THE STORY of DEAF PILOT NELLIE ZABEL WILLHITE

Dreams Take Flight

By Brittany Richman
Illustrated by Alisha Monnin

Published by Sleeping Bear Press™

When Nellie Zabel was born, nature sang outside her window.

A robin called, *tut-tut, tut-tut*.

Wind rattled oak leaves.

But when Nellie turned four, everything changed. As she lay in bed, her mother wiped her fevered forehead and fussed over her spotted skin. Nellie's fever rose. And then . . . sounds stopped.

Nellie may not have been able to hear, but her mother wouldn't give up on her. She knew her daughter could do anything. She taught her to stitch, cook, and feed the cattle. But Nellie dreamed of more. She watched in wonder as robins soared across the cloudless sky. She dreamed of doing something just as extraordinary.

Nellie's mother showed her a new way to communicate: through her hands. She formed Nellie's fingers into shapes—special motions for any word Nellie needed: hungry . . . home . . . love.

Speaking through sign language opened Nellie's world. She smiled up at her mother. Yes, maybe now she *could* do anything.

But soon a sadness weighed on her heart deeper than anything she'd ever known: losing her mother. Nellie sobbed into her father's shoulder. What would she do now?

Nellie knew her father wondered the same thing. He wasn't prepared to care for her alone. Regular schools wouldn't take a deaf child. Her father did the only thing he could: he sent Nellie to a school for the deaf many miles away.

On her first day, Nellie's nerves felt like a bird fluttering inside her stomach. But she had an opportunity not every deaf child got: a chance to learn with kids just like her. For the first time since her mother passed away, hope spread its wings.

Nellie couldn't wait to make friends. But when she tried speaking to the other students with her hands, the teachers refused to allow it. Nellie felt ashamed. In 1905, sign language was seen as hindering rather than helping deaf students. Her teachers wanted her to use only her mouth to speak. But how could she say words she couldn't hear? Nellie's hope plummeted.

Despite the strict rules, Nellie approached each new day with a smile. It didn't take long for Nellie's determined spirit to capture the hearts of two of her teachers, Dr. and Mrs. Mead. Because her father lived so far away, they brought her home as a foster child.

Nellie, if you can communicate, you can do anything, they told her.

Mrs. Mead taught Nellie to read lips by watching people's mouths open and close as they formed words. Nellie soaked it up. And she practiced speaking back by feeling the air tickle her throat as she projected her voice.

With this new discovery, Nellie's heart took flight once again. Could she really do anything? Nellie believed maybe she could.

When Nellie was older, she worked as a typist all across South Dakota, assisting government officials. She was soon recommended for a job at the airport near Sioux Falls.

As Nellie filed papers and sorted forms, she gazed out her window . . . and saw something incredible.

A biplane soared and spiraled through the cloudless sky. It rippled across the air. As it flew close to the building, vibrations rumbled beneath her feet, sending shivers up her legs. Nellie watched in awe and wondered, what would it be like up there, free and flying like the robins she loved?

For weeks, Nellie watched planes come and go. Deliveries. Drop-offs. Daring dives.

Her boss noticed the careful way Nellie organized the office and paid attention to detail. He saw someone smart and capable—someone who could do anything.

One day, he saw her smiling at the sky.

"Nellie, why don't you take lessons?" he said.

"Me? Fly?" Nellie responded.

"You'd be the first woman pilot in South Dakota," he said. "Think about it."

From that moment on, Nellie couldn't stop thinking about it. For weeks, she paced her office wondering, *Could I? Should I? Do I dare?*

Not long afterward, Nellie saw a flyer for flight lessons posted near her office. Her heart nearly skipped a beat.

A few weeks later, on a gray November day, Nellie showed up at the airport for her first flying lesson! A chill spread through the air but excitement warmed her through.

Before Nellie could fly, she had to learn all about the flight instruments: turn indicators, oil pressure and fuel gauges, and compasses. There was so much to learn.

Soon it was time to go up in the air. Nellie tried to watch her instructor's every move. But there was one problem. In 1927, cockpits opened wide, with one seat in front of the other. The instructor sat up front, the student in the back—and urgent commands were shouted over the buzz of the plane. If Nellie couldn't see his face, how would she know if something went wrong?

She tried to remember everything she'd learned. But when she thought about flying herself, Nellie's mind filled with doubt. No deaf person had ever received a pilot's license before. She could do a lot of things . . . but could she really fly?

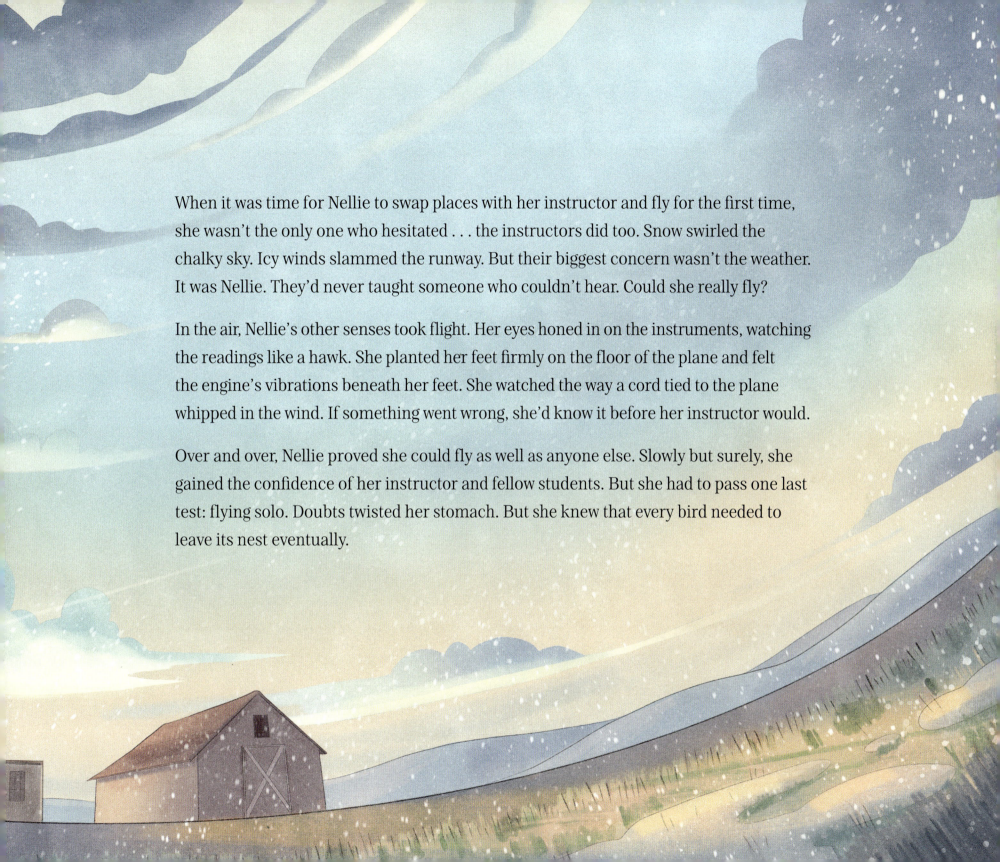

When it was time for Nellie to swap places with her instructor and fly for the first time, she wasn't the only one who hesitated . . . the instructors did too. Snow swirled the chalky sky. Icy winds slammed the runway. But their biggest concern wasn't the weather. It was Nellie. They'd never taught someone who couldn't hear. Could she really fly?

In the air, Nellie's other senses took flight. Her eyes honed in on the instruments, watching the readings like a hawk. She planted her feet firmly on the floor of the plane and felt the engine's vibrations beneath her feet. She watched the way a cord tied to the plane whipped in the wind. If something went wrong, she'd know it before her instructor would.

Over and over, Nellie proved she could fly as well as anyone else. Slowly but surely, she gained the confidence of her instructor and fellow students. But she had to pass one last test: flying solo. Doubts twisted her stomach. But she knew that every bird needed to leave its nest eventually.

Soon came the day for Nellie's solo flight. She boarded the open cockpit, took a deep breath, and strapped her helmet to her chin, her curls flapping in the breeze. *Come on, Nellie*, she told herself. *You've flown before, plenty of times.*

In the air, the icy wind whipped at her cheeks, reddened from the cold. Nellie shivered—but not from the temperature. The thrill of being alone in the air, flying so free, was unlike anything Nellie had felt before. Her eyes peered across the bluest sky of the entire winter. She thought of her mother, her father, her foster parents, all she had overcome. And she remembered . . .

I. Can. Do. Anything. Nellie knew it with her whole soul.

Nellie gazed down at the other students, now the size of ants. They waved up at her, urging her to brave the landing.

Nellie double-checked her surroundings. She circled the landing field over and over. She felt the engine purr beneath her feet. She couldn't mess this up. There might not be another chance.

Finally, Nellie maneuvered the plane into position. She spotted her instructor waving her in, then circled around and pointed the nose downward.

As Nellie touched down into a perfect three-point landing, an arc of icy water sprayed up from her wheels.

Nellie sighed with relief, then hopped down from the plane with a smile as wide as her hometown prairie. Her instructor and fellow students surrounded her, whooping and hollering and slapping her on the back with pride.

"You did it, Nellie!" said her instructor. "You're the first female pilot in South Dakota."

Later, a letter arrived in the mail: Nellie's pilot's license.
She was now the first deaf licensed pilot in the entire country.

Nellie gazed across the South Dakota prairie. A breeze rippled the branches of a nearby oak tree, tangling Nellie's curls and carrying a robin's song through the air.

And although she couldn't hear it, she knew better than most what it was like to fly like one.

Note About the Research

My family often travels through Rapid City, South Dakota's small regional airport. Just before the security gate, there's a picture of a young woman: Nellie Zabel Willhite. She's hard to miss with her spunky grin and dark curls pouring from her aviator's cap. After a friend finally encouraged me to look her up, I quickly realized Nellie deserved way more than just a picture in an airport. Because of my own deaf ear, I instantly felt a special connection with Nellie and was deeply inspired by her attitude of not letting anything hold her back.

As with many stories from history, there's no way of knowing every detail about Nellie's life, such as specific conversations. I tried to piece together the unknowns the best I could with information that was available. I gathered fragments of her life from old newspapers, letters, and interviews, each piece revealing a clearer picture of who she was and the extraordinary life she led.

More About Nellie

Nellie Zabel Willhite was born on November 22, 1892, in Box Elder, South Dakota. Her mother died shortly after her father returned from the Spanish-American War in 1898. At the time, deaf children were often misunderstood, seen as a burden and sometimes sent to institutions for the mentally ill. Luckily, Nellie's father had the foresight not to do that. Instead, he sent her to the nearest school for the deaf—in Sioux Falls, about a five-hour drive from Nellie's home. Unfortunately, during the late 19th and early 20th centuries, the deaf population was often seen as less capable than the hearing population. Thankfully, Nellie had courageous adults in her corner who loved her and taught her to thrive, despite her lack of hearing.

When Nellie became the first female pilot in South Dakota, at age 35, and the nation's first deaf licensed pilot, she stirred up a lot of attention—not all of it positive. Many criticized her for endangering others or for even having the audacity to attempt to fly at all. Nellie

Credit: South Dakota State Historical Society

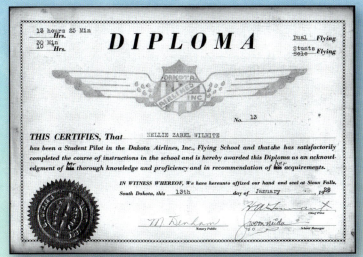

Credit: South Dakota State Historical Society

herself said, "I think the women were a little envious, and the men, too, especially after I got so much attention." Nellie also faced discrimination and was often passed over for jobs because she was a woman and deaf. She was also paid far less than male pilots.

Nellie became a talented stunt pilot, flying daring acrobatics in air shows and goodwill tours across the U.S. She also became a charter member of the "99 Club"—an organization started by Amelia Earhart for female pilots. For a while, she owned her own plane (named "Bard"), obtained her transport license, and, until 1944, worked as a commercial pilot, carrying airmail. As she went from town to town, she often delivered messages from government officials, dropping the messages in parachutes toward the intended destination.

Credit: South Dakota State Historical Society

Shortly before she died in 1991, at the age of 98, She was inducted into the South Dakota Aviation Hall of Fame. She also inspired plays and was included in the International Aerospace Womens Association in 1991.

Her photos now line the hallway of the South Dakota School for the Deaf in Sioux Falls—the very school Nellie attended over 100 years ago—inspiring other young students to what's possible in their own lives.

Sources

Daniel, Dorinda. "Nellie Zabel Willhite: The State's First Female Pilot." South Dakota Historical Society Foundation. 2021.

Pitlick, Wendy. "Nellie Willhite Was First Female Pilot in State, First Deaf Pilot in Country." *Black Hills Pioneer*, 2008.

Miller, Scott. Personal communication with author, 2023. Historian, South Dakota School for the Deaf, Sioux Falls, South Dakota.

Huetter, Ted. "Flying Deaf." *Museum of Flight* (blog), 2023.

Bunjer, Lori. Western Highways: *Journeys through Space and Time*. Sioux Falls, SD: Augustana College, 2021.

Willhite, Nellie Zabel. Transcription of Interview. South Dakota Historical Society. 1985.

Willhite, Nellie Zabel. Letters to Charles Zabel. Center for Western Studies, Augustana College, Sioux Falls, South Dakota, 1904[EN]1934.

To James, Liv, and Lincoln: Dream BIG!

—Brittany

For My Mother

—Alisha

Text Copyright © 2025 Brittany Richman
Illustration Copyright © 2025 Alisha Monnin
Design Copyright © 2025 Sleeping Bear Press

Sleeping Bear Press is an imprint of Cherry Lake Publishing Group.

Publisher expressly prohibits the use of this work in connection with the development of any software program, including, without limitation, training a machine learning or generative artificial intelligence (AI) system.

All rights reserved.
No part of this book may be reproduced in any manner without the express written consent of the publisher, except in the case of brief excerpts in critical reviews and articles. All inquiries should be addressed to:

SLEEPING BEAR PRESS™

2395 South Huron Parkway, Suite 200, Ann Arbor, MI 48104
www.sleepingbearpress.com © Sleeping Bear Press

Printed and bound in South Korea
10 9 8 7 6 5 4 3 2 1

Library of Congress Control Number: 2025010936
ISBN: 978-1-53411-355-8